Learn Peace –
Live Peace

by S. Albert Newman

RoseDog Books

PITTSBURGH, PENNSYLVANIA 15238

RoseDog Books
585 Alpha Drive
Suite 103
Pittsburgh, PA 15238
Visit our website at www.rosedogbookstore.com

ISBN: 978-1-4809-6290-3
eISBN: 978-1-4809-6312-2

This book is dedicated to the memory of all those whose lives have been taken by gun violence. As the Franciscans pray, "May the Lord give you peace."

Peace, My Brother

Peace, My Sister

Peace, My Soul

From "Amazing Peace," a Christmas poem by Maya Angelou

Acknowledgments

This book resulted from the sacrifice of my wife, Corinne. She knows what it is to be a "book widow" for the time of this writing.

With much love, Albert

Chapter One

"There are two reasons to fight evil in the world—
one is to change it, the other is to make sure it does
not change you."

William Sloan Coffin Jr.[1]

That we live in a violent world and country scarcely needs to be documented. On July 18, 1984, at a McDonald's in San Ysidro, California, twenty-one people were shot and killed; on August 19, 1987, sixteen children were shot and killed in a school in Hangerford, England; on April 20, 1959, thirty-five people were shot and killed in Port Arthur, Australia; on April 28, 1996, thirteen high school students were shot and killed at Columbine High School in Littleton, Colorado; on April 16, 2007, thirty-two students were killed on the campus of Virginia Tech University in Blacksburg, Virginia; on November 5, 2009, thirteen people were killed at Fort Hood, Texas; on July 22, 2012, sixty-nine people were gunned down in Utoya, Norway; on July 29, 2012, twelve people were killed in a movie theater in Aurora, Colorado; on August 5, 2012, six people were killed as they sought to enter a house of worship in Oak Creek, Wisconsin; on December 14, 2012, twenty beautiful children and six adults were killed in the school massacre in Sandy Hook, Connecticut[2]; on May 28, 2014, nine people were shot and killed on the campus of the University of California[3] in Santa Barbara; twelve people were shot and killed in the Naval Yard in Washington, D.C.; in 2012 five hundred people were shot and killed in the city of Chicago, Illinois; and twelve people were shot while watching a neighborhood basketball game on September 16, 2013, also in Chicago— and the tragedies go on.

In a nation where there are now more guns than people[4], I would suggest the wild present has become much more dangerous than the Wild West of olden days. Such levels of violence require moral action by those who care about and value human life.

There is a moral if not genetic thread that connects all of us as human beings. The loss of even one life diminishes us all. The person who could cure cancer, the one could become a great artist, the one who could design the most wonderful buildings, the one who could lead us to the discovery of literally new worlds may be the one whose life is taken. Humanity cannot afford these subtractions.

To be sure, to someone on the East Coast, the loss of a student or teacher in Colorado may seem distant and far away, yet the one who is killed may well be our relative, our son or daughter, our parent or friend. As William Coffin suggests, the evil of gun violence needs to be changed before the evil of gun violence changes us.[5]

In these pages, you are challenged to listen to these "teachers of peace," to consider thoughtfully the human and moral consequences of gun violence in our nation and world. Surely the numbers must speak to us. NOW is the time for improvement and change.

Chapter Two
Albert Schweitzer

"We die by what we eat and drink but more we die by what we think."

Edward Arlington Robinson[1]

One of the most impressive voices for peace in the past century was Dr. Albert Schweitzer. In the closing remarks of his speech on receiving the Nobel Peace Prize in Oslo, Norway, on November 4, 1954, Schweitzer challenged "all people to take the first step along a new path." He called for "a rise in the reflective" [thoughtfulness], a profound ethical will that leads to a new and genuine culture." In words so incisive for our time, he calls for "a new conclusive RENAISSANCE, which brings peace to the world."[2]

The word "renaissance" refers to a new way of thinking, a new set of values, a change and reorientation of life and living, the adoption of a new set of goals and priorities.[3] In history, "renaissance" refers to that period in which there was a rise from the "dark ages," an awakening, a period of new insight with an accent on education, with a new stimulus to artistic creation and expression, on new ways and directions for economic progress and development.

Schweitzer wrote: "A new renaissance must come, one much greater than that from which we stepped out of the Middle Ages. It must be a renovation in which mankind discovers that the ethical is the highest truth and the highest practicality."[4] He seeks a new renaissance (a new way of thinking) that brings peace to the world.

Schweitzer is best known for the phrase "reverence for life." Biographers and commentators point to the association of Schweitzer's thought to Eastern and Indian influences, which underscore the unity of all things, a "reverence" for ALL forms of life. For Schweitzer, ethics and human thought about what is right and wrong includes both human beings and EVERY LIVING CREATURE. He states "ethics" includes a spiritual and HUMANE relationship with both people and all living creatures.[5]

Intellectually and educationally, Schweitzer commands respect and deserves to be heard. He earned a Ph.D. in Philosophy, a Th.D. in Theology (New Testament and Biblical Studies), and a Doctorate in Music (he was a world-famous organist, organ builder, and composer). Learning of the plight of African people with little or no access to medical treatment or care, Schweitzer left his position as Professor of Philosophy at the University of Strasbourg and went to medical school, becoming a physician and going to Labarene (now known as Ghabon) to establish a hospital and provide medical care to the native people.[6]

Schweitzer is relevant. Gun in hand or not, he calls for new ways of thinking—for a recognition of the sacredness of all life, for healing and not hurting, for PEACE and nonviolence as a new pattern of human behavior. His call for a new "renaissance"—for a whole new way of thinking—makes him a true prophet for our time

The word "renaissance" comes from the French language and literally refers to "a new birth." Just as newborn infants open their eyes and see for the first time, so Schweitzer challenges us to come alive, to see life with clearer moral vision.

In history, renaissance was "a coming alive," seeing the beauty and potential of what life can be. At the time of the Renaissance, there was a new optimism; old and stagnant ways of doing things were abandoned. Literally new continents (new worlds) were discovered. New ways of constructing buildings were adopted (the great cathedrals of Europe date from this period as does the voyage of Christopher Columbus). From the Renaissance, new books came to be printed and published, universities were established, astronomy began to develop, and there was great progress in the fields of medicine, painting, sculpture, music, and the fine arts. The Renaissance was literally a time of COMING ALIVE, of a new birth to those life possibilities that can make for a better world.

Ethically, Schweitzer's call for "a new renaissance that leads to peace" is a challenge for us to come alive to something better than the culture of gun violence and death. The numbers are DEPLORABLE. More than ONE MILLION people have died by gunfire in the United States since 1968.[7] Schweitzer challenges us to come alive to PEACE as a new and better way. Schweitzer challenges us to OPEN OUR EYES to new life possibilities: helping and not hurting, lifting and not putting down, being positive and not negative, spreading kindness and not hatred, bringing smiles and not frowns, laughter and not tears, joy and not sadness, helpfulness and not neglect, beauty and not blemish, unity and not division, harmony and not discord, peace and not violence, and life enhancement and not destruction. The Danish philosopher and theologian Soren Kierkegaard once said, "Why are you content to live in the cellar when there are rooms upstairs?"[8] Why are we content with current levels of killing and gun violence? Is it moral to say that gun violence is okay as long as it is not my child or my relative who is the victim? Albert Schweitzer calls us to come alive to a better way that certainly can be. No other nation on the face of the earth matches the United States in levels of gun violence and death. Albert Schweitzer calls us to something better, to improvement and change.

People who are lost in a forest want more than anything to find a way out. Dr. Albert Schweitzer prompts us to open our eyes and to see a new and better world, to turn our eyes in the direction of art and music, science, and self-giving as a way out of the dangers of a gun-saturated environment. He calls for new ways of living that lead to urban safety and peace.

Chapter Three
The Quakers

"Peace is the only battle worth waging."

Albert Camus[1]

The Gospel of John, the Fourth Gospel of the Christian tradition, declares that "the True Light which enlightens everyone, was coming into the world."[2] This verse came to be called "the Quaker text"[3] because it affirms the basic Quaker understanding of human nature. According to the Quakers, every human being is of eternal value because each of us has an inward capacity for God-relatedness and spiritual receptivity, a capacity to receive and experience the Inner Light of the Creator God.

In his early life, the young cobbler-apprentice and sometimes shepherd, George Fox, was troubled in his search for religious insight and meaning. The externals of religious practice in the churches of his day were perceived as being outward, shallow, and unsatisfying, as failing to bring any sense of peace in mind or spirit. Then one day as he was walking in the countryside of his native England, Fox was overcome by a sense of the spiritual, by the conviction that every man [human being] [4] is capable of God-relatedness and spiritual visitation. In his JOURNAL, Fox wrote of "that of God in every man [human being]." It was his conviction that every person is given "the

Light of Life," that every person is to be valued and treasured because we are connected to and given the "Light from above." For Quakers, the very fact of being aware of the light of the mind (consciousness) is evidence of human value and spiritual potentiality. Since every person has this "Light from God"[5], just living and being human means that every life is both sacred and valuable. This Inner Light that is in everyone is therefore the basis and underpinning of the Commandment "THOU SHALT NOT KILL." Quakers teach us that we should never put out the light, which is the divine gift in every living person.

Quaker anthropology or understanding of who we are as human beings tells us that every person is a bearer of the Light of God. The belief that every person possesses the Light of God (regardless of race or skin color) was also the basis for the antislavery (abolitionist) perspective of Quakers.[6] ALL PEOPLE ARE VALUABLE. All have within them the Light, which comes from God. This is the ultimate reason for restraint.

When a weapon is pointed at another human being, Quakers remind us there is something sacred about that person. Life has a divine origin, an ultimate value, a never-diminished dimension. This recognition of the sacredness of human life is the Quaker reason not to hurt or harm or destroy a human life—not that of ourselves or of others.

How and what we think about the value of another living human being greatly determines how we act to preserve and protect a life, which Quakers believe truly comes from God. Quakers affirm that everyone is unique, unduplicated, as varied as snowflakes, of eternal value and potential. The "Light which enlightens every person" is never to be put out. To be human is to be precious.

Chapter Four
Walt Whitman

'There never was a good war or a bad peace."
Benjamin Franklin[1]

Walt Whitman (1819-1892) was the American poet first credited with the almost prose style of writing known as "free verse," a poetic style of expression, almost a stream-of-consciousness way of writing. Whitman was a poet, a newspaper editor, a person who supported himself at various times in his life as a carpenter, a printer, and a schoolteacher, as well as serving as a payroll clerk for the U.S. Army, an employee of the U.S. Indian Bureau, and an office worker in the service of the U.S. Attorney General.[2] Yet it was his work as a volunteer nurse during the American Civil War that provided the impetus for his peaceful and most antiwar expressions.[3]

Whitman describes himself in one poem as 'THE WOUND DRESSER," as a counselor and consoler of the dying. Given its proximity to his place of employment in Washington, D.C., Whitman may well have served as both a hospital and battlefield nurse with those wounded in the Battle of Antietam (September 16-18, 1862). These days are often said to have been the most horrible days of warfare in American history. In only TWO DAYS of fighting, there were 23,000 casualties—people either captured, wounded, or killed.[4]

In the poem "Song of Myself," Whitman reveals his role as "The Wound Dresser":

To anyone dying, thither I speed...
Let the physicians and priests go home....
I am he bringing help for the sick as they
pant on their backs...[5]
Bearing the bandages, water and sponge,
straight and swift to my wounded I go,
Where they lie on the ground after the battle brought in,
Where their priceless blood reddens the grass, the ground.
Or to rows of the hospital tent, or under the roofed hospital,
To bring rows of cots up and down each side I return,
To each and all one after another I draw near,
Not one do I miss...
Onward I go, I stop. With hinged knees and steady hands to dress
wounds, I am firm with each, and the pangs are sharp yet
unavoidable, One turns to me, his appealing eyes—
poor boy!
I never knew you. Yet I think I could not refuse this moment
to die for you, if that would save you.
Come sweet death! Be persuaded O Beautiful death! In mercy
come quickly!
I dress the perforated shoulder, the foot with bullet wound,
one with gnawing and putrid gangarene, so sickining, so
offensive....the hurt and wounded I pacify with soothing hand...
I sit by the restless all the dark night, some are so young,
some suffer so much. I recall the experience sweet and sad.[6]

To the violence and tragedy of the Civil War (in which 625,000 lives were lost) must be added the shocking totals from America's involvement in its

MANY other conflicts. There were 116,516 Americans killed in World War I; 405,424 were killed in World War II; 36,516 in the Korean Conflict; 47,424 were killed in Vietnam; 3,220 were lost on September 11, 2001; 6,717 Americans were killed in the Iraq War and Afghanistan—and there are more casualties each day and each passing month.[7]

These staggering numbers of American lives lost in the insanities of war should be a perpetual warning and a primary impetus in the search for PEACE. Whitman's antiwar sentiments stem directly from his aversion to the suffering and gore resulting from armed conflict. As Benjamin Franklin said, "There never was a good war or a bad peace."

It was none other than the five-star General Omar Bradley who said, "It is folly to argue that one weapon is more immoral than another, for in the larger sense it is WAR itself that is immoral and the stigma of such immorality must rest upon the nation which initiates hostilities."[8] The violence of government-sanctioned war engenders hatred and division and lessens our horror at the taking of the life of another. Warfare prompts feelings of revenge and retribution, of killing and violence as a way to resolve human differences. As Mahatma Gandhi said, "An eye for an eye only ends up making the whole world blind."[9]

From his firsthand experiences of the pain and horrors of war, Walt Whitman was convinced that life is for living, not to be wasted in those times when hostility and despair triumph over hope and the joyous possibilities of a new day.

Chapter Five
The Rev. Dr. Martin Luther King Jr.

"How wonderful it is that nobody needs to wait a single
moment before starting to improve the world."

Anne Frank[1]

Rabbi Abraham Joshua Heschel once said that Martin Luther King Jr. represented "a voice, a vision, a way"[2]—a voice of one who became a central leader in the struggle for racial justice in America, a voice that is still the envy of every would-be speaker or public leader (deep, strong, cadenced, captivating). Dr. King was a voice for the downtrodden and oppressed people, first in the South, then for the entire nation and world.

From the time of his leadership in the bus boycott in Montgomery, Alabama, until his brutal assassination in Memphis, Tennessee, on April 4, 1968, Dr. King practiced the way of nonviolent resistance, confrontation, and protest. This nonviolence is said by some to be an echo of the nonviolent methods Mahatma Gandhi employed in the struggle for the independence of India from the colonial rule of Great Britain. Though Dr. King acknowledged Gandhi's influence on his thought, King's nonviolent methods can best be seen as an outgrowth of his own understanding and experience of the Christian faith.

Martin Luther King was a son, a grandson, a great-grandson, and a nephew of Christian ministers. Though he once described his faith as an inherited faith, his beliefs and practice of faith were grounded in a living, personal relationship with a companion God.[3]

In a time of deep personal struggle, early in the bus boycott in Montgomery, Dr. King's faith became very real and personal:

> *Sitting at a kitchin table late at night I discovered that religion had to be real for me, that I had to know God for myself. And I bowed down over a cup of coffee and I prayed a prayer out loud. I said, "Lord, I'm down here trying to do what is right. But Lord, I am losing my courage. And I can't let the people see me like this because if they see me weak and losing my courage, they also will begin to get weak." Then it happened and it seemed at that moment that I could hear an inner voice saying to me, "Martin Luther, stand up for righteousness, stand up for truth...and Lo I will be with you even till the end of the world." I heard a voice of Jesus saying "still fight on." He promised never to leave me alone.[4]*

That experience, that vision in the kitchen, gave King new strength. He said, "Almost at once my fears began to go, my uncertainty disappeared."[5]

In his courageous yet dangerous quest for racial justice, through his outspoken witness against the war in Vietnam, to his final support of economic fairness and justice in Memphis, Dr. King was a leader with a "voice," a "vision," marking a clear path toward racial justice and equality. In his own words, he was a "drum major for justice, a drum major for PEACE, a drum major for righteousness."[6]

While Dr. King was a powerful witness to people in his own time, he continues to be a moral spokesman for us and even for generations yet to come. He was a man of peace who both preached and practiced the ways of nonviolence, non-retribution, and self-control in the face of great hostility and bitter opposition.

As a nation, we rightfully celebrate the day of his birth as a day of PEACE, as a day devoted to thought and meditation as to what is moral and right, as to what contributes to public safety and the establishment of a good and wholesome community. In this regard, the King Holiday is unique—a day rightfully devoted to how life in the community, the household, the city, the nation can be improved.

It is shocking that since the gun death of President John F. Kennedy in 1963, since the gun death of his brother Robert in 1968, since the gun death of Dr. King in 1968, ONE MILLION PEOPLE have died from gunshots in the United States.[7]

Dr. King preached and still wants to teach the ways of PEACE. As he said: "We must learn to live together as brothers and sisters or we will all perish together as fools."[8]

The Rev. Dr. Martin Luther King Jr. was and IS a TEACHER OF PEACE. He both lived and died pleading for all people to realize their highest potential by making the dream of peace their most hopeful and consistent choice. The old hymn declares that God has placed the world in OUR hands, that we have the power to make the world a garden of life and PEACE or we can tarnish both the world and ourselves when we and the guns we possess become instruments of injury, sorrow, and death.

Were he alive today, Dr. King would still be pleading for nonviolence and PEACE—in our homes, in theaters, in our streets, in places where we work, between races, sexes, and nations. He would say, "PUT YOUR GUNS DOWN, GAIN A HIGHER VISION, LIVE IN PEACE."

Dr. King not only dreamed of a better world, he preached and spoke and witnessed to what that better world can be. Dr. King is and should be remembered as a powerful speaker. Among his many assets and strengths was his ability to attract the attention, the allegiance, the ardent following of young people. In their very formative years, even teenagers were captivated by the rightfulness of his cause, by his costly commitment to peace. Again, we should note the tragedy of his loss. No one has come on the scene of American moral discourse who can even approach his power of persuasion, the appropriateness of his message, the Pied-Piper dimensions of his leadership.

A gun, a hate-and-violence-consumed person, robbed the world of the most influential witness and TEACHER of PEACE America has ever produced.

Chapter Six

Guns in the Home

"The whole purpose of life is to make a world that is safe
and good for children."
>
> Attributed to Professor William Lyons Phelps
>
> of Yale University

When you hold a gun in your hand, when you aim it at someone, when that gun is fired, horror, sadness, death, and regret can come as surely and as fast as a bullet can travel.

In the late seventies, when I was serving as pastor of a church in Northern New Jersey, the stark consequences of having a gun or guns in the home became all too clear. Both parents were working, usually not returning to the home until 5:30 or 6:00 P.M. The father in the family felt the need to protect his family by keeping a loaded handgun in the nightstand in the bedroom of his home. The teenage son came home from school. He wanted to show the gun to his best friend, who had come over for an after-school visit. IT HAPPENED.

Certainly by accident, certainly by gun-storage irresponsibility, the son shot and killed his best friend. One life was taken. Many lives were changed forever. Grief was piled upon grief. Permanent scars were left in the mind and soul of the shooter.

Statistics show there is at least a forty-percent greater chance of a friend or family member being shot in a home where there are weapons than there is of shooting or harming an intruder.[1] The price of keeping an unsecured gun or guns in a home can be enormous.

The tragic consequences of such an incident cannot be reversed. After the fact is much too late. Regrets do not wipe away very real tears. We need to ask the question: "Do the benefits really outweigh the tragic consequences that can happen when guns are owned or improperly stored or secured?" What if it were your son or daughter injured or killed in such a gun incident? The time for preventive action must come before such a tragedy.

Think about these numbers: Thirty-five people are killed by gun violence each day in the United States. Fifty people take their own life each day by gunfire. One hundred twenty-five people are injured by gunfire each day in America.[2] Are guns in the home really worth this amount of hurt and loss? Multiply these numbers by 365 days in a year, and the price of gun ownership becomes even more horrific. That's 12,775 people per year killed by gun violence. That's 18,250 suicides by gunfire each year. That's 45,625 people injured by gunfire each year in America. Twelve thousand seven hundred seventy-five people killed by gun violence each year. That is more than THREE 9/11's —the result of gun violence each year in the America. ARE GUNS REALLY WORTH THIS AMOUNT OF HUMAN TRAGEDY AND LOSS?

One of the verses of the Civil Rights song "We Shall Overcome" expresses the hope, the belief that "We shall live in peace, someday. Oh, I do believe, we shall live in peace someday." The dream of this song will never come about as long as we in America continue to value the right and liberty of gun possession over the right of all of us to live out our natural lives free from the threat and tragedy of gun violence.

Chapter Seven
St. Francis of Assisi

"And Jesus went about doing good."

Acts 10:38[1]

The man who came to be called "Saint Francis" was born in the small Tuscan town of Assisi in the year 1181. At birth he was given the name of Giovanni (John) Bernadone, though he soon came to be called "Francisco" or "that little Frenchman," and the name Francis stayed with him throughout his life and history.[2]

His father was a moderately wealthy cloth merchant. As a youth, it is said that Francis was gallant, witty, dashing, joyous, and habitually spending lavishly—delighting in fine clothes. He loved riding horseback and hiking. When still quite young, Francis joined the provincial army of his day and went off to war. Somewhere in his wandering, Francis heard the voice of God telling him to "rebuild My Church." Taking these words literally, Francis set himself to the task of rebuilding a small stone chapel in Assisi. The New Testament story of Jesus talking to the "rich young ruler" (Luke 18:18-22)[3] spoke to Francis in a very personal and powerful way: "And Jesus said 'Go and sell all that you have and give it to the poor and come and follow Me.'" Embracing poverty ("Lady Poverty is my bride") as a lifelong pattern of living, Francis lived simply, wandering the byways and preaching as he travelled. He once said, "It is no use walking anywhere to preach unless the walking is also our preaching,"[4] and even more powerfully, "Preach the Gospel at all times and when necessary use words."[5]

Francis and his followers called themselves "God's Troubadours" or "God's Minstrels—people who went about performing skits, playing instruments, singing, and seeking to bring smiles and joy to those around them.[6]

In his wandering, Francis delighted in the world of nature. He would commune with dancing springs of water. He delighted in his friend: the fire. Francis loved to greet the sun as it rose. This love of nature found expression in his "Canticle of the Sun"[7]—a deeply felt song of praise to the God of all creation:

Praise be my Lord God for all creatures,
especially for our brother sun,
who brings us the day and who brings us light;
fair is he and shines with a very great splendor,
O Lord, he signifies You to us.
Praise be my Lord for our sister the Moon,
and for all the stars, which you set clear and
lovely in Heaven,
Praise be my Lord for our brother the wind,
and for air and cloud, calm and all weather
by which you uphold life in all creatures,
Praise be my Lord for our sister water,
who is very useful to us and humble
and precious and clear.
Praise be my Lord for our brother fire,
through whom you give us light in darkness
and he is very bright and pleasant
and very mighty and strong.
Praise be my Lord for our Mother the earth

which sustains and keeps and brings forth many diverse fruits
and flowers of many colors and grass.

From his involvement and love of nature, Francis suggests the world of art, music, poetry, literature, and perhaps even the world of science as human endeavors that provide positive options to paths and patterns of violence, hatred, and harm.

Francis, revered for his Chistocentric faith, his mysticism, his sacrificial and devoted life, and his LOVE OF NATURE, was declared "The Patron Saint of Ecology" by Pope John Paul[8] on November 29, 1979. Often depicted with a bird in his hand or on his shoulder, Francis provides a model for those who seek both peace and purpose in relishing the beauty and restorative powers of the surrounding world. His life example reminds us that a song, a poem, a painting, and a scientific inquiry into the world of nature are positive alternatives to conflict, division, hurt, and hate.

Francis is to be treasured for his wonder and even worshipful appreciation of the everyday and simple things that surround us. Francis is a teacher of peace in the way he lived his life, demonstrating for us the great gift of personal freedom and the power of self-determination. Francis could have been a merchant, a warrior, an attorney (as his father wanted him to be)[9], a teacher, a playboy, or an ambitious and many splendored cleric, yet he models for us the unique human power of self-determination, the ability to mold and shape our lives as we feel inwardly led and guided to do. Said another way, Francis had the courage to live his dream, to follow the inward light and impetus of mind that caused him to go about sharing love and joy to everyone he chanced to meet. This was his philosophy of life. This is his guiding example.

How different this is from following paths of violence, hatred, and hurt. We do well to remember that we each have, for better or worse, a life vision or philosophy of life that determines our values and direction in life. As human beings, we can have a high vision or a low one, we can choose the high road or the low. Francis chose to shape his life by filling all of his moments with the joy and thrill of sharing moment by moment the love that

God inspires. It is by no means a coincidence that the newly elected pope of the Roman Catholic Church chose the name "FRANCIS,"[10] saying again in our time that the earthing and sharing of God's love is life's highest purpose and God's intention for us all.

In the storms and turbulence that buffet every life, Francis found something solid to hold on to, always seeking to make life better for everyone he chanced to meet. Like his Lord, Francis "went about doing good." This is different from living a grasping self-oriented life, different from those who go about dispensing violence, bullying, and spewing hostility and negativity wherever they happen to be. Francis reminds us that we are here for helpfulness, for kindness, for sharing the love, the smiles, the joy that God intends.

Francis is a superlative life teacher in that he not only loved the world of nature, he loved PEOPLE. Embracing lepers, the most despised and rejected people of his day, Francis adopted a greeting for everyone, for every creature and person he happened to meet—saying to each one (either silently or out loud), "May the Lord give you peace."[11] What a challenging alternative, a greeting and prayer for everyone we meet. Such a practice elevates the mind and sets the tone for positive and caring interaction. This is worth a try, greeting every person we meet by saying and praying, "May the Lord give you peace."

This prayer is attributed to Francis:

> *Lord, make me an instrument of Your Peace.*
> *Where there is hatred, let me sow Love;*
> *Where there is injury, Pardon,*
> *Where there is doubt, Faith;*
> *Where there is despair, Hope;*
> *Where there is darkness, Light;*
> *Where there is sadness, Joy;*
> *O Divine Master, grant that I may not seek so much*
> *to be consoled as to console,*
> *to be understood as to understand,*
> *to be loved as to love*

For it is in giving that we receive,
It is in pardoning that we are pardoned,
and it is in dying that we are born to eternal life.[12]

Detractors have criticized Francis for his attitude toward money. Some see this as an impractical if not impossible ideal. Yet it must be said that Francis embraced and practiced poverty only to accent his conviction that LOVE is the most important thing in the world, more important than wealth, status, or property. In his practice of everyday human affirmation, in his practice of seeking to bring smiles, gentleness, and encouragement to everyone he met, Francis captured the essence of the Christian dynamic, the effort to fill all of the days, hours, and moments of life with God's love made real.

The life example of Saint Francis is instructive in the way he found his life purpose in kindness, his life joy in immersing himself in the wonders of nature, and his life riches in seeking to bring help and even moments of happiness to everyone he happened to meet.

Chapter Eight
The Hutterites

The Sixth Commandment: "Thou Shalt
Not Kill"[1]

While the Hutterite community has been featured on a recent television series, my first exposure to members of the group came during a series of events seeking a moratorium on the death penalty in New York State during Mario Cuomo's years as governor. The Hutterites participated in large numbers, affirming their belief in nonviolence and peace.

The Hutterites trace their founding to the year 1528 and the Anabaptist movement accompanying the Protestant Reformation.[2] The Anabaptists were so called because of their rejection of the practice of infant baptism and membership in a state or all-inclusive church organization. The other Anabaptist groups remaining in the United States are the Mennonites and the Swiss Anabaptists, which includes the Old Order Amish. Instead of wanting to reform the medieval Church, the Anabaptists wanted entirely to withdraw from its influence and to establish smaller, voluntary church groups based on shared beliefs and mutual economic concerns.

Religiously the Hutterites wanted to establish what they called "colonies from Heaven" (Philippians 3:20 refers). Biblically the phrase refers to the way in which ancient Roman colonies were established in distant and sometimes unfriendly lands. The colonies, though distant from Rome, practiced Roman Law and customs even though they were located in distant and sometimes hostile environments. Hence the Hutterites sought to establish groups or colonies where HEAVEN'S ways were practiced even in a worldly and sometimes contrary surrounding.

The group derives its name from Jacob Hutter of Tyrol in Moravia. Though not the founder of the group, Hutter was an early member whose devotion and ardor intensified the group's practices and beliefs. Jacob Hutter was one of the group's first martyrs, being persecuted and burned at the stake for his beliefs in 1536.[3]

Hutterites first came to North America in 1874, establishing the first colonies in what are now the Dakotas, Montana, and the Hudson River Valley of New York State. Another significant migration (in 1918) established colonies in Canada, this group settling in Canada rather than the United States in protest of military conscription (the draft) at the time of the First World War.[4]

Hutterites believe in sharing all things, shunning individual ownership of all properties, farm equipment, houses, vehicles, farm animals, and crops. Hutterites shun all forms of violent conflict and confrontation, objecting most vigorously to combatant roles or forced military involvement. Hutterites strictly obey the Biblical admonition "Thou Shalt NOT Kill," agreeing to serve only as conscientious objectors in times of war.

Life for Hutterites focuses on COMMUNITY. All things are to be shared by members of the colony (the "Bruderhof"). All work, all decisions are to be made FOR THE GOOD OF THE COMMUNITY. The ethical question for everyone and at all times becomes "How can I, how can we make life better for everyone—for children, for neighbors, for everyone we meet, at all times and in all places?" This Hutterite concentration is worth repeating: "How can I make life good for everyone? What is good for the community, for the country, for the world, for the planet? Is my action helping to build a good, a better, more life-sustaining place in which to work and live? Are my actions helping to establish a better place for children and adults?"

While the Hutterites live their lives in a predominately rural and agrarian setting, it is instructive to translate their values to a more urban, even inner-city environment, asking the ethical question "What can I, what can we do to make life better for people in this apartment building, on this block, in this neighborhood, on this street where I work and live, where my children play and go to school?"

Hutterites are early risers, greeting each new day with a firm resolve to do all they can to ENHANCE life in and for the community. The lifestyle and values of the Hutterites are instructive. They concentrate their energies on community improvement. Translated to an urban setting, is it not better to build parks, to plant flowers and gardens, to compete for safety and cleanliness, to do all that can be done for community enhancement rather than ignoring situations that contribute to community blight and deterioration?

Hutterites are teachers of peace, always seeking the positive for their families, for their neighbors, and for their communities. Together they "pull the rope" in one direction, seeking life-enhancement and community improvement in a climate of mutual affirmation and peace.

Chapter Nine

The Writing of St. Paul[1] Romans 12:9-18

"Thy word is a lamp to my feet and a light to my path."

Psalm 119:105

In today's world, attitudes toward the Bible are both interesting and perplexing. A recent television series on the Bible has captured an astonishing amount of interest, yet largely gone is a prevailing attitude of heartfelt allegiance, acceptance, and almost worshipful attentiveness and devotion. This being said, it is still my hunch that there is in America a residual respect for the words and teachings of the scriptures. Someway most people seem to think the words of the Bible should and do matter.

In "pondering peace," the words of the Bible from the writings of Paul should be considered. Paul has been called the first and greatest Christian teacher and missionary. He travelled throughout the known world of his day, sharing his beliefs, his vision of love (First Corinthians 13 contains his great "Hymn to Love"), and his understanding of how human beings are to relate to one another (especially as he wrote what we now know as the twelfth chapter of the Book of Romans).

In this letter to the Christian community at Rome, Paul wrote, "Let your love for one another be 'genuine'...the real thing. Hate what is evil...hold fast to what is good...be aglow in the spirit...contribute to the needs of people, provide a home for the homeless...live in harmony with one another...don't pay back an evil with another evil...fill your mind with noble thoughts...and IN SO FAR AS IT DEPENDS ON YOU, LIVE PEACEABLY WITH ALL" (Romans 12:9-18). Live in peace with other nations, with people you like, with people you may not like, with people you agree with, and even with people with whom you may disagree.

The words that are capitalized are intended to guide human beings in their relationships with one another. "IN AS MUCH AS IT DEPENDS ON YOU, LIVE IN PEACE WITH ALL PEOPLE." These words are "in the Book." The Bible teaches that when there is a choice, when it is at all possible, the ways and pathways of PEACE are to be chosen.

Following the Second World War, the United States changed the name of one of its largest segments of government from the "WAR Department" to the "Defense Department," following the spirit of this Biblical insight and teaching. "As long as it depends on you, live in PEACE with everyone."

As a teacher of peace, St. Paul emphasizes individual responsibility. He says in effect that the peace of the world, of the city, nation, and our homes, is in our hands. He reminds us that we find peace for ourselves when we live in peace with others. Paul says in effect, "Don't start a fight, a conflict, a battle, a war. When there is even the slightest possibility, choose a peaceful way."

In international relationships, in places of work, in schoolrooms, on playgrounds, when driving a motor vehicle, in our homes—when you can find a peaceful way, choose peace. "In as much as it depends on you [and it does] live peaceably with everyone." These words are not so much a demand as they are wise counsel and an invitation to a better life. If necessary to keep the peace, walk away from a fight, "turn the other cheek" (Luke 6:29). "Shaloam" in Hebrew, Eirene or Erene in Greek refers to the best possible state of being for us and for all. A translation might be "BLESSED" or "HAPPY" are you when you seek peace, when you give this kind of gift as a life possibility to another person.

The Bible teaches that PEACE is God's best and happiest vision for us as individuals, for us in our relationships with other religions, races, ages, genders, and nations. Paul says, "Live in harmony with one another....do not repay an evil with another evil but rather meet and overcome evil with good." This may not come naturally or be easy, but this is God's way for a better life and community.

Chapter Ten
Ms. Betty Williams

"Do you enrich the world or impoverish it?"

Eli Wiesel in *Legends of Our Time*[1]

The peace affirmations and contributions of Ms. Betty Williams, the 1976 Nobel Peace Prize winner (with co-recipient Mairead Corrigan), provide instruction and inspiration. On August 10, 1976, Ms. Williams witnessed an automobile accident involving an Irish woman, Ms. Anne Maguire, and three Maguire children. Mr. Danny Lennon, a member of the Irish Republican Army, had been shot by British authorities, his car going awry, hitting the Maguire car, and killing the three children. Betty Williams stopped her car and tried to render aid.[2]

For Betty Williams, the accident was a tipping point: Too many bombs, too many shootings, far too much violence had occurred in the war ("The Troubles") between Protestants and Catholics, the Irish and the British, the rulers and the ruled. Within two days of the accident, Betty Williams and Mairead Corrigan (Anne Maguire's sister) organized a peace march to the graves, Catholics and Protestants joined together in the march, the united effort bridging years of violence, hatred, and division.[3] Two weeks later, Betty Williams and Mairead Corrigan organized another march with over

35,000 previously divided people taking part. Betty and Mairead then formed the Women for Peace Movement, which later became the more inclusive Community for Peace People.[4]

The first declaration of the Peace People organization includes these precepts:

- We want to live and love and build a just and peaceful society.
- We want for our children, as we want for ourselves, our lives at home, at work and at play, to be lives of joy and peace.
- We recognize that there are many problems in our society which are a source of conflict and violence.
- We recognize that every bullet fired and every exploding bomb make that work for peace more difficult.
- We dedicate ourselves to working with our neighbors near and far, day in and day out, to build that peaceful society in which the tragedies we have known are a bad memory and a continuing warning.[5]

Betty Williams and Mairead Corrigan changed the deplorable violence of their time into an active determination to work and witness for PEACE. Interestingly, they first organized WOMEN to begin their protest, bridging deep and longstanding divisions with their realization that "ENOUGH IS ENOUGH. Together we must work for a better day."

The question must be asked: When do WE reach a tipping point? When does the shooting, the killing, and the violence in our nation become too much? "WHEN IS ENOUGH ENOUGH?" We need to remember that FIFTY people die from gun suicide each day in America. Thirty-five people die each day in America in situations where people shoot at each other. We need to remember that one hundred twenty-five people are INJURED by gunfire each day in America.[6] Consider the violence of our cities: Seventy-four people were shot in the city of Chicago in only four days of the 2014 Fourth of July weekend.[7] Betty Williams and Mairead Corrigan realized in their hearts and minds that "ENOUGH IS ENOUGH," and they began a massive action that led to peace.

As difficult as it seems, we need to remember that the Constitution of the United States both has been and can be amended and corrected. The Twenty-First Amendment changed and corrected the Eighteenth Amendment (which established prohibition).[8] When circumstances change, changes can be made to reflect both modern inventions and the needs of society. The technology of gun manufacture has radically changed since the time of the writing of the Second Amendment. It is a gross misunderstanding of both science and history to think the Second Amendment writers envisioned AK-47-type rifles or rapid-fire automatic pistols. At BEST, it probably took at least five minutes between single shots from the muzzle-loading weapons, which were state of the art at the time the Second Amendment was written. The laws of our nation have not kept pace with developments in gun technology.

Is it not possible to write an amendment to the Constitution that would allow for responsible gun ownership while restricting public access to large-capacity rapid-fire weapons?

Could not such an amendment deal with access control, the registration and transfer of ALL weapons while providing reasonable restrictions for those who have been or are currently undergoing treatment for mental illness, such restrictions likewise including those with past criminal (felony) convictions? Is there not enough wisdom to write laws that truly provide for domestic tranquility, promote the general welfare, and secure the blessings of life and liberty for us and our posterity?   (language reminiscent of the Preamble to the Constitution)

Against very high odds, Betty Williams and Mairead Corrigan began a movement that led to peace. It has truthfully been said that "we will have a better world when we truly want one," when people of courage join together to act to create communities and homes where PEACE is seen as the better vision and pattern for human relationships. "Do we enrich the world or impoverish it?"

Chapter Eleven
Carolyn McCarthy

"It is never right to harm a man [human being]."

Socrates

Quoted by Elton Trueblood, *The Life We Prize.*

Harper & Brothers. New York: 1951 (p. 114)

On December 7, 1993, as a train pulled into the Merillon Avenue Station on Long Island, New York, a man by the name of Colin Ferguson pulled out a 9mm Ruger automatic pistol and began firing at passengers. Ferguson shot and killed six people and seriously injured nineteen others. On this terrible day, Carolyn McCarthy's husband, Dennis, was killed and her son, Kevin, was seriously wounded.[1]

Carolyn McCarthy could easily have folded her hands, bowed her head in grief, and spent her remaining years in sorrow and self-pity. Rather, she too said, "ENOUGH IS ENOUGH," and began a campaign for gun control by running for Congress as a member of the House of Representatives of New York's Fourth Congressional District.[2]

In 1997 she sponsored a bill in Congress requiring trigger locks on all weapons. Congresswoman McCarthy also introduced legislation banning the sale of guns to tourists and to all other nonresidents of the United States. In the aftermath of the Columbine High School shootings in Colorado, she introduced legislation requiring all firearms to be child-resistant.

Following the Virginia Tech shootings in April 2007, Carolyn McCarthy again spoke of the need to further prevent gun violence, specifically calling for more screening and background checks and testing the mental health of those seeking to purchase weapons in any state of the nation.[3]

After the Federal Assault Weapons Ban expired in September 2004, Congresswoman McCarthy introduced a measure to reauthorize and strengthen the bill, seeking to ban any semiautomatic rifle, shotgun or handgun "originally designed for military or law enforcement use, and any weapon that is not particularly suitable for sporting purposes as determined by the Attorney General of the United States."[4]

The Second Amendment to the Constitution of the United States speaks of "the right to bear arms." As a matter of public health and safety in apartments or homes, in seeking to establish safer streets and schools, cities, and neighborhoods, all of us need to assess the morality, wisdom, and necessity of gun ownership and use. Do guns in almost every hand (it is said there are now more guns in the United States than there are people) produce a SAFER place for children, for passengers on planes, buses, and trains? In very recent news, a three-year-old child shot and killed a one-year-old. In New Haven, Connecticut, a one-year-old child was shot while being held in the arms of her aunt on the front porch of their home. Is this how people in our nation are supposed to live? Is this how people in our nation are supposed to die? As Carolyn McCarthy has asked, "WHEN IS ENOUGH ENOUGH?"

When guns are owned, when guns are in hand, the idea of "CONSEQUENTIAL ETHICS" should come to mind. What are the consequences of carelessness? What are the consequences of revenge, hatred, of seeking to get even? What are the consequences of gun possession in cases of domestic violence and hostility? What are the consequences of gun access for those who are mentally ill? There is even the question, what are the consequences of gun misuse to the shooter or shooters? Colin Ferguson escaped the death penalty for his crimes only because New York State did not have a death penalty bill when he shot and murdered six people and injured nineteen others, yet he was sentenced to THREE HUNDRED FIFTEEN YEARS in Attica Prison for his crimes.[6]

The right to shoot, harm, or kill another human being is limited. Murder, the taking of another human life, is against the law in every state of the union—in every city, town, school, theater, street, or place of residence. "The right to bear arms" is by no means a license to kill except in very clear and limited circumstances of self-defense. Aiming or shooting a gun at another human being has consequences. A piece of lead is hurled at that person with tremendous velocity. There are moral, legal, and physical consequences when a gun is fired at another human being. The jails and prisons of America are filled with people with regrets, with people who wish they had acted with more restraint, and with people who wish they had preserved their own freedom and had saved the life or lives of others.

Ethical thinkers from Moses to Socrates have reasoned "Thou Shalt Not Kill"[7] and "It is never right to harm a man [human being]."[8] It cannot be proved or disproved, but it may be that there is a scar, a mark on the eternal soul of every person who wantonly takes the life of another.

Chapter Twelve
"The Golden Rule"

"Once to every man and nation comes the moment to decide. In the strife of TRUTH and falsehood, for the good or evil side."

James Russell Lowell, 1845

I know of a household that owns a very fine set of china. Wanting to protect it, the set is placed on a shelf in the basement and never used. The "Golden Rule" may very well be like this set of fine china. It is there. It is "on the books." Maybe some have heard of it. But is it used? Is it brought out, dusted off, consulted, taken in, followed, and made a rule and guide for life?

The words are few: "Do unto others as you would have them do unto you."[1] Expressed in the negative: "Don't do to others what you would not want them to do to you." Said another way: "Treat other people as you yourself want to be treated." The words and teachings come from Jesus in the "Sermon on the Mount" (Matthew 7:12 and Luke 6:31).

The J. C. Penney Company got its start as "The Golden Rule Store." Mr. Penney's personal motto and rule for doing business was to treat every customer as "you" would want to be treated. The store rose from a one-store beginning to a national empire. "The Golden Rule" is still taught and commended to its executives and employees. "Treat other people as you want others to treat you."

The Sermon on the Mount in the Gospel of Matthew ends with this word of caution and wisdom: "Everyone who hears these words and does them is like the wise person who built his house on a ROCK. The rains came, the winds blew, but the house did not fall" (Matthew 7:24). The teaching is this: The "Golden Rule" is ROCK SOLID. "TREAT OTHER PEOPLE AS YOU WANT TO BE TREATED."

The words of the Golden Rule are simple, yet when guns are considered, when a gun is in your hand, how would you want to be treated? How would you want your children to be treated?

Like that set of fine china, the Golden Rule needs to be taken out of the basement of memory and be used as a guide. When it comes to the management and use of guns, let this rule be your guide: "Treat other people as you would want to be treated."

It is unfortunately true that many in our society grow up in an ethical vacuum. Family relationships are fractured. There are too few dinner conversations about what is right and wrong, healthy and fair. Grandparents (who can serve as ethical teachers) frequently live at great distances from core families. Schools (especially public schools) may be afraid to teach or even touch on ethical considerations. The question of "whose ethics shall we teach?" frequently leads to the conclusion that we will therefore not teach or discuss ethics at all.

Churches, where one would think ethics would be taught and communicated, are weakened by fragmentation and division. Churches, in many cases, have become ethical creampuffs, seeking more to entertain than to be confrontational or controversial. Bad ethics (such as clergy child abuse) can lead to ethical deafness and widespread inattention to ethical considerations. It is unlikely that gun violence will be reduced until ways are found for basic ethics to be more effectively taught and communicated. As a start, THE GOLDEN RULE needs to be brought out, learned, internalized, and lived by. Following this rule can lead to PEACE.

Chapter Thirteen

Newtown

Prayers for Comfort - Prayers for Peace

On December 14, 2012, my wife and I happened to be in Newtown, Connecticut, for a family visit. When we drove into town, police cars were everywhere. We first thought of a terrible motor vehicle accident, then perhaps a bank robbery. When we arrived, we knew nothing about what had happened at the Sandy Hook Elementary School. News quickly came that there had been an incident at the school, less than a mile from where we were visiting. At first the numbers were few, then came the horrible truth. Twenty first-grade students and six educators had been killed. These were beautiful people, dedicated teachers, a talented principal, beautiful, beautiful children full of smiles, joy, and the wonderful possibilities of life. The event created seismic waves in the community, state, nation, and world.

The incident raised a multitude of issues:

(1) GRIEF: Parents, grandparents, and people near and far were shaken to their foundations. As many as three funeral services a day was the norm for more than a week. Valiant and faithful clergy did what they could to provide a presence, some care, some comfort, and hope for the families.

(2) THE ISSUE OF GUN TYPE AND AVAILABILITY: A military-type semiautomatic weapon with a large-capacity magazine was used to kill TWENTY-SIX people in less than five minutes elapsed time. Does such a weapon originally designed for military-combat use have any purpose in a highly populated, supposedly peaceful community?

(3) GUN STORAGE: The Newtown shooter had ready access to what some would consider an arsenal of weapons: rifles, pistols, a shotgun, and a semiautomatic high-capacity rapid-fire weapon. The issue of gun access and proper storage and security looms very large in this incident.

(4) MENTAL HEALTH AND GUNS: By any assessment, the shooter in the Newtown massacre was mentally troubled and disturbed. In response to the Tucson, Newtown, Aurora, Virginia Tech, and the University of California, Santa Barbara, mass shootings, the question of who should be able to purchase or handle a gun is most evident. Mental illness is difficult to define. At times it seems there are more questions than answers. What types of mental illness lead to violence? How does society restrict gun ownership in light of permissive interpretations of "the right to bear arms"? The stigma of mental illness causes both individuals and families to hide mental pathologies. It is feared that jobs can be lost. Promotions can be forfeited, and access to educational opportunities can be denied. People feel mental illness must be hidden. The stigma of mental illness is antithetical to any system of background checks yet to be set forth. The right to personal and medical confidentiality seems to preclude revealing factors that might possibly prevent gun ownership, possession, or use.

While there may be no way absolutely to prevent gun violence from the hands of those who are mentally ill, the first line of prevention, if at all possible, must rest with CAREGIVERS.

The first priority of parents, families, physicians, teachers, clergy, and friends of those who are struggling with mental illness—depression, excessive fatigue (posttraumatic-stress disorders), drug or alcohol addiction, schizophrenia, or narcissism—needs to be WATCHFULNESS, followed by cautious and effective intervention. Where there is a potential for faulty judgment, preventing access to weapons ought to be the first thought and action of caregivers. Prevention depends on DISARMING those who might be a source of harm to themselves or others. It is far better to err on the side of caution than it is to face the tragic consequences of guns in wrong or troubled hands.

Preventing guns from being in the possession of the mentally ill or troubled is a complex matter. Some propose to limit gun purchases for those who have been legally (by a court) declared to be mentally ill. This proposal seems to leave open a wide area of possible concern. It is highly likely that there are many who are mentally disturbed and lacking in judgment who have NOT been legally identified. Such persons may even be in the majority. The psychiatrist William Minninger once stated that mental illness does not affect just one in five people or two or three in five people. "Mental illness at some point affects FIVE out of FIVE people."[2] It would be helpful if those in the counseling, Psychological, and psychiatric professions could be freed from confidentiality requirements and be more directive with their client patients, legally identifying those who should not have access to weapons.

Caregivers, friends, and family members usually have some insight and information as to those who might pose a danger to themselves or others. Where possible, such knowledge or even suspicion should lead to an active intervention, changing the familiar quotation "If you know something, DO SOMETHING" to separate guns from the hands of the troubled.

GUNS IN THE WRONG HANDS—this is the source of danger. All Americans need to remember that we are talking about instruments that can and do cause the death of over 30,000 people each year in the United States. A requirement to record all gun sales and all gun transfers seems reasonable when both personal and public safety is at risk. At a minimum, questions need to be asked about past criminal involvement or convictions and about any history of mental illness or condition (medications and/or treatment). With gun rights should come gun responsibility.

Just since the horrible tragedy at Newtown, over 5,000 Americans have lost their lives as a result of gun possession and misuse (all this in less than five months' elapsed time). Even more shocking is the fact that since the death of John Lennon on June 8, 1980, over 1,080,000 people have lost their lives by gunfire. Morality and public safety clearly call for something better, for some improvement and change. Inaction, resignation, and allowing the number of guns in the United States to multiply and multiply do not solve the problem. If there were a scourge, an epidemic, some natural disaster causing the death of so many, there would be a clear demand for action. Ethical blindness and inertia allow far too many to die, and as Newtown so vividly reminds us, some are our nation's most beautiful people, even our children.

Chapter Fourteen
Parenting for Peace

The "Selishter Rebbe" said to Eli one day: Be careful with words, they are dangerous. Be wary of them. They beget either demons or angels. Nothing is as dangerous as giving free rein to words."[1]

The Christmas story from the Christian tradition conveys the message that the peace of the world begins at the cradle. How we parent our children determines not only their tranquility of mind and spirit but their developing attitudes, which can make for peace with others. Perhaps even before birth, we begin to "bend the twig" in ways that can influence a child's disposition toward either harmony or hostility.

The agricultural imagery is appropriate. The gardener or farmer who is concerned for the health and optimum development of a plant nourishes and tends the plant with gentleness and care. It is unheard of for the good farmer to kick or abuse a seedling. Plants will grow as they are cared for and tended. Some growers even say it is good to talk nicely to or even sing songs to plants if they are to grow and develop to their maximum beauty and fruitfulness. Peace in the home and in families-yet-to-be depends on providing a surrounding atmosphere of tenderness and care from a child's earliest days.

47

Consider these actions and options that nourish children in peace:

1. MODEL PEACE IN THE HOME:
    Make HARMONY a goal for your family. Every family member can add or subtract from the family treasury of peace. Peace is the result of careful choices. We either build peace or we tear it down by the way we act and interact with one another in families.

2. CHOOSE WORDS CAREFULLY; THEY DO MATTER:
    Both the tone and the content of family communications are factors in the cultivation of peace or its opposite. The latter half of the old saying "Sticks and stones may break my bones, but words will never hurt me" just is not true. The choice of words and the choice of word tones can determine the future peace of mind and the quality of human relationships for family members and especially for our children. The words we choose can be like poison, or they can yield both joy and peace way around the bend of the future for our children.

3. CHOOSE AND SHARE HEROES AND HEROINES OF KINDNESS AND PEACE:
    While every newspaper and newscast seemingly overflows with BAD news—murders, rapes, riots, ravages of weather, wars, and conflicts—THERE ARE STORIES OF HUMAN KINDNESS AND CARE. Share and tell these stories: a young woman shares a kidney with someone she doesn't even know, an auto body shop insists on donations for a food pantry prior to paying for a repair, thousands of meals are shared each day and each week by food pantries and food centers, meals are shared in homes where sorrow has come, people volunteer to share their knowledge and gifts in tutoring (teaching reading, math, and science to those who need a hand-up in these areas of learning), and people who build houses for other people. Habitat for Humanity is a good example of such sharing.

CHOOSE HEROES AND HEROINES WHOSE ACTIONS MAKE FOR PEACE. Share these stories. They paint pictures of the positive, and they communicate those things that make for peace. The seeds of kindness can blossom and grow.

4. HELP CHILDREN TO LEARN ABOUT ANGER:
    Anger can be a healthy and appropriate emotion. It is okay to be angry when others hurt or harm. The Bible even says, "Be angry but sin not" (Ephesians 4:26). The Bible, especially the Old Testament, is full of examples when even God is pictured as being angry at the disobedience and God-forgetfulness of people who are supposed to know better. Anger is a gift when it leads to improvement and correction. Anger motivated by a desire for retaliation and revenge only multiplies division, separation, and harm. Peace depends on TRANSFORMATION. Anger can be transformed by FORGIVENESS. The hot-tempered impulse to smack your enemies is transformed by the challenge to "love your enemies" and to "do good to those who despise you" (Matthew 5:44). There is the Biblical challenge to transform the "slap on the cheek" by "turning the other cheek," to transform injury and hurt by the miracle and magic of a reciprocating kindness and affection.

    As a young man, I enjoyed throwing rocks into a pond. I'd throw them high in the air, and the stone created circles and rings that went out from the point of impact all the way to the edge of the pond. This memory provides an example of the peace-generating potential of forgiveness when kindness is allowed to transform hostility, when love is chosen as a response to insult and injury. The Bible also reminds us that we can leave vengeance and revenge to God. God will even the score so we don't have to (Romans 12:19). Insight as to the control and management of anger is a vital ingredient in parenting for peace.

5. In parenting for peace, TEACH THE BEST OF RELIGIOUS
    TRADITION.
    Share insight as to how to VALUE OTHER HUMAN BEINGS.
    Share the "Golden Rule." Share the challenge of transforming anger
    with kindness and love. Share the insight of St. Paul that "in as
    much as it depends on you, live in peace with all people" (Romans
    12:18).

6. KISSES AND HUGS:
    Kisses and hugs need to be part of the teaching of peace from a child's
    earliest days. The psychologist Virginia Stair has written, "We need
    FOUR hugs a day for survival. We need EIGHT hugs a day for health.
    We need TWELVE hugs a day to thrive and grow in happiness."[2]

7. EDUCATION:
    Survey after survey points to the crucial role that parents play (or
    fail to play) in the EDUCATION OF CHILDREN. Parental inter-
    action with teachers needs to be an ongoing reality. Parents helping
    with homework and parents monitoring progress in learning is
    foundational to guided growth in the educational process. The tril-
    ogy of TEACHER, SCHOOL, and CHILD needs to be consistently
    expanded by the involvement of PARENTS. Parents can also influ-
    ence their children by their OWN continuation in learning. View-
    ing education as a lifelong process provides children with both a
    positive example and incentive for their growth and development.
    The ability of children to learn and to KEEP ON LEARNING en-
    sures the child's best pathway to future stability and optimum self-
    care. People who are growing and traveling in a positive direction
    don't have time to engage in the negatives of hostility and violence.

8. MUSIC AND THE ARTS:
    It has been said that "MUSIC tames the savage beast."[3] Sharing the
    classics and sharing the best of the world of art points to the sur-

rounding gifts of nature, which both calm and elevate the human spirit. John Erskine once said, "Music is the only language in which you cannot say a mean or sarcastic thing."[4] Music at best is an experience of psychic and spiritual receptivity, a way of experiencing at our deepest levels the mystical gifts intended for the elevation of the human spirit. Said another way, music has the power to lift minds above conflicts, the power to literally "change minds," replacing hostility with psychic harmony and the desire for peace. Music is medicine for the soul. Even the dour and pessimistic Frederick Nietzsche could say, "Without music life would be a mistake."[5] From lullabies to concerts, the sharing of music is both a joyous opportunity for parents and a pathway to the cultivation of peace.

The peace of communities and the peace of the world begins at the cradle. Is anything more important than transmitting the gift of PEACE to the next-and-coming generation? We are concerned to teach mathematics and science and the intricacies of computers and Smartphones to our children. As parents, how much more do we need to be TEACHERS OF PEACE?

Chapter Fifteen
A Children's Story[1]

"All things bright and beautiful, all creatures great and small, all things wise and wonderful, the Good Lord made them all."[2]

Cassie:	Robert, did you know that the word "STORY" is related to the word "HISTORY"? You just drop the first two letters and you have "STORY."
Robert:	I get it. I like stories. They tell us about ourselves and how we got to be the people we are.
Cassie:	What do you think about "DREAMS"? Do they tell us about ourselves?
Robert:	They can. They also can tell us about the future... about how we want things to be. I sometimes dream about a delicious ice cream cone. On a HOT day, that is something I want to happen.
Cassie:	A long time ago, in the Bible, a man by the name of Isaiah had a dream about how things can be. He dreamed about PEACE...about the way things can be among people.

Robert:	Tell me about that. How can things be? How can things be better?
Cassie:	Isaiah's dream is a great vision of PEACE...about how things should be in a KINGDOM OF PEACE. He dreamed:

In the kingdom of peace the wicked wolf will lie down with the lamb. The leopard will lie down with the young goat. Little calves will feed with young lions and even little children will be among them to care for them.

Isaiah dreams BIG. In this kingdom of PEACE, this is how things can be:

Cows and bears will eat together. They will lie down and rest together in peace. Lions will eat straw like cattle. Even a poisonous snake will not hurt or harm a little child.

In this dream about how things can be:

There will be nothing harmful or evil and all the earth will be covered in God's peace as the waters cover the sea.

Robert:	I get it. Nobody will hurt anybody. You said that dreams tell us how things can be. NOBODY HURTING ANYBODY. That's the dream God gave to Isaiah a long time ago. It's a truth-story about how God wants things to be...on my street, at my school, in my town, in every city, between my country and yours.

This story is based on the vision of the "PEACEABLE KINGDOM" as this vision is told in Isaiah 11:6-9. It is a story about how even bitter enemies can change so they begin to live together in PEACE. This dream-story communicates God's intention for the human family. Any act of hatred and violence subtracts from the peaceful world that God intends.

In the story that Catholic people tell of the Miracle of Lourdes (France), the Blessed Mother Mary is said to have appeared to three shepherd children on the thirteenth day of each month, from May through October, 1917. In one of these visions, Mary is said to have said, "Peace is needed."[3] What Mary said is the truth for cities, for schools, for shopping centers, for theaters, for college campuses, for nations and people of different races, genders, and beliefs. "And there shall be nothing harmful or hurtful, hateful or evil in the world that God intends. And the earth will be covered in God's peace as the waters cover the sea."

Chapter Sixteen
Think about These Words

"May he who causes peace to reign in the High Heavens
let peace descend on us, on all Israel, and on all the world."[1]

"Jesus said to Peter in The Garden of Gethsemane: 'Peter, put up your sword.'"[2]

Charles Jeffreys (1807-1865): "Let only those who would make a quarrel be the ones to fight."[3]

Mother Teresa: The Simple Faith: "Silence is Prayer, Prayer is Faith, Faith is Love, Love is Service, the Fruit of Service is Peace."[4]

St. Augustine: "We must shape the outer world according to an inward vision."[5]

Tim Russert: "The Best exercise for the human heart is to reach down and pick someone else up."[6]

John Wesley: "Do all the good you can, to all the people you can, in all the ways you can, for as long as ever you can."[7]

St. Francis of Assisi: "It is not fitting when in God's service to have a gloomy face or a chilling outlook."[8]

Jesus said: "Blessed are the PEACEMAKERS for they shall be called `Children of God.'"[9]

Dr. Martin Luther King Jr.: "Life's most important, persistent and urgent question is 'What are you doing for others?'"[10]

John Lennon: "If everyone demanded PEACE rather than a television set there would be peace."[11]

Supreme Court Justice Anthony Kennedy: "Everybody has a right to do many things but the important question is 'What is the right thing to do?'"[12] (This statement has much to say about "The Right to Bear Arms." We may have the Right to Bear Arms, but what is the RIGHT and SAFE THING TO DO?)

S. Albert Newman: "It is impossible to drift into something better, to stumble into a better world by accident. The good must be chosen, pursued, made a conscious, deliberate and life-persistent goal."

John Lennon: "Imagine all the people living life in peace. You may say I'm a dreamer, but I'm not the only one. I hope someday you'll join us, and the world will be as one."[13]

William Targ: "The trouble with the publishing business is that too many people with half a mind to write a book...DO."[14]

S. Albert Newman: "We avoid the negatives of life (drugs, alcohol, depression, hostility, wasting, withering) only when we realize that we want something else more and we set ourselves single-mindedly to gaining that something else."

S. Albert Newman: "We die when we refuse to choose a pathway (a plan) for living."

S. Albert Newman: "Don't be a victim of the poverty of purpose and identity."

Isaiah 2:2-4: "And it shall come to pass that the mountain of the Lord's house shall be   established on the top of the mountain... and nations shall flow into it...and God will teach us His ways and we will walk in His paths...and God will judge among the nations and shall rebuke many people and they shall beat their swords into plowshares and their spears into pruning hooks, nations shall not lift up sword against nation, neither shall they learn war anymore."[15]

"Be ye kind one to another."[16]

Dr. Peter Marshall: "A different world cannot be built by indifferent people."[17]

Dr. Peter Marshall: "Give us a clear vision that we may know where to stand and what to stand for, because unless we stand for something, we shall fall for anything."[18]

Anonymous: "A person all wrapped up in him/herself makes a very small package."

Mother Teresa: "How can you say there are too many children? This is like saying there are too many flowers." (Consider the migration of over 60,000 children from South and Central America to the United States.)[19]

S. Albert Newman: "When you are seeing only the bleak, the dark, the negative...you are not seeing correctly."

Anonymous: "Every day God makes silk purses out of sow's ears."[20]

Dag Hammarskjold: "God does not die on the day when we cease to believe in a personal deity, but we die on the day when our lives cease to be illuminated by a steady radiance, renewed daily, of a wonder the source of which is beyond all reason."[21]

Mahatma Gandhi: "Nonviolence is not a garment to be put on and off at will. Its seat is in the heart and must be an inseparable part of our very being."[22]

Governor Mario Cuomo: "There are only two commandments in Hebrew: (1) to "love your neighbor" and (2) "to repair the universe."[23]

Nelson Mandela: "Education is the most powerful weapon you can use to change the world."[24]

Piers Morgan: "We cannot keep our homes and our children safe in America because there are too many guns in too many hands."[25]

Willam Gladstone: "We look forward to the time when the Power of Love will replace the Love of Power. Then will the world know the blessings of PEACE."[26]

Mother Teresa: "I will never understand all the good that a simple smile can accomplish."[27]

An Old Italian Proverb: "We are all like wounded birds with only one wing. Unless we cling to each other and share, we cannot fly."

Notes

Chapter One
Introduction

1. William Sloan Coffin Jr. Flyer, "Keeping The Faith, Sustaining Activism For The Long Haul." Skidmore College, Saratoga. New York: January 26, 1991.
2. *Time Magazine*, January 14, 2013, pp. 14-15.
3. *The Hartford Courant*, June 13, 2014, Editorial.
4. The Census. gov. estimated the population of the United States in 2009 as being 308 million. *Time Magazine*, "The Gun Fighters," January 28, 2013, estimates the number of firearms in the United States at 310 million. *Time* states: "As of 2009 there were more guns in the United States than people." p. 32.
5. Coffin, op. cit.

Chapter Two
Albert Schweitzer

1. Quoted in Robert Frost, *The Early Years*. Holt, Reinhart and Winstron, New York: p. 215.
2. *A Treasury of Albert Schweitzer*, edited by Thomas Kiernan, The Citadel Press, New York: Second Printing, January 1966, pp. 224-225.

3. *Webster Unabridged Dictionary.* The word "renaissance" has as its root the French word meaning "rebirth," a new way of thinking and being.

4. Dr. Schweitzer, *Pilgrimage To Humanity,* translated by Walter Stevermann, University of Tulsa, published by Philosophical Library Inc., New York: 1961, p. 76.

5. *A Treasury of Albert Schweitzer,* op. cit. p. 74.

6. *Pilgrimage To Humanity,* op. cit. pp. 20-31.

7. Article by Mark Shields, *Tampa Bay Times,* January 18, 2013, states there have been 1,384,171 gun-related deaths in the United States since 1968. THIS IS MORE THAN THE NUMBER KILLED IN ALL THE WARS IN AMERICAN HISTORY (1,171,177), according to this article.

8. Soren Kierkegaard, quoted by Carlyle Marney, *Faith in Conflict,* Abingdon Press, New York, Nashville: 1952, p. 116.

Chapter Three:
The Quakers

1. Albert Camua, *Significance of The Stranger,* goodreads.com. /quotes.

2. Gospel of John, Chapter One, Verse Nine.

3. Journal of George Fox, 1952 publication.

4. Journal of Fox, op. cit.

5. Gospel of John, op. cit.

6. John Woolman, the tailor, journalist, preacher, merchant, is the Quaker most associated with the abolitionist movement. In 1754 he published his treatise "Some Considerations About the Keeping of Negroes." Woolman was known to refuse to sit at a table with slave keepers (owners). *Wikipedia, The Free Encyclopedia,* John Woolman (1720-1772).

Chapter Four
Walt Whitman

1. Benjamin Franklin quote: *Bartlett Familiar Quotations,* John Bartlett, Little Brown and Company, Boston, Toronto, Tenth Edition. Franklin letter to Josiah Quincy, September 11, 1773, p. 331 Bartlett.

2. Whitman, *Selected, With Introduction by Leslie A. Fiedler,* General Ed-

itor Richard Wilbur, Dell Publishing Company, Inc., New York: 1959, pp. 24-25.

3. CNN Report, September 16, 2012, also *The Hartford Courant,* September 16, 2012, Section B, pp. 1-3, "Connecticut Soldier In The Fury, America's Bloodiest Day."

4. Ibid.

5. Whitman, Leslie Fiedler, op. cit. pp. 118-121.

6. Ibid. pp. 119-121.

7. *United States Casualties in War,* Wikipedia. Org.

8. Bradley quote by David McCullough, *TRUMAN,* Simon and Shuster, New York, London: p. 761.

9. Mahatma Gandhi, Brainy Quotes.

Chapter Five

The Rev. Dr. Martin Luther King Jr.

1. "Anne Frank Quotes," Brainy Quotes, Google Custom Search, "Single Moment Before."

2. *We Shall Overcome,* edited by Peter J. Albert and Robert Hoffman, Pantheon Books, a division of Random House, Inc. 1980, p. 7.

3. Ibid. pp. 220.

4. Ibid. p. 20. The words "Never, No Never Leave Me Alone" echo the words of an old and familiar Christian hymn,

5. Ibid.

6. Words later inscribed on his monument in Washington, D. C. Quoted in *The Autobiography of Martin Luther King, Jr.,* edited by Clayborne Carson, Intellectual Properties Management, Inc., in association with Warner Books, A Time Warner Company, Avenue of the Americas, New York: 1978, p. 366.

7. Reported by Piers Morgan, CNN News, January 6, 2013.

8. The Martin Luther King, Jr. Research and Education Institute, *Quotes on War and Peace,* p. 1, Stanford edu/index, php/resources/articles/ King, "Remaining Awake Through A Great Revolution," p. 3 of 6.

Chapter Six

Guns in the Home

1. It is estimated that guns kept in the home to protect against an intruder are 43 times more likely to kill a family member, friend, or acquaintance than they are to kill an intruder. From The Children's Defense Fund, April 24, 2013. (Google search) and Noah Schreiber, "Yes, Really Ban Guns." July 24, 2012, referencing "the Kilman Study." New England Journal of Medicine.

2. Numbers reported by Piers Morgan. CNN News, following the killing of seven people and the wounding of thirteen more on the campus of The University of California at Santa Barbara on May 23, 2014.

Chapter Seven

Saint Francis of Assisi

1. Acts 10:38.

2. Williston Walker, *A History Of The Christian Church.* Scribner's Sons, New York: 1959, pp. 234-236.

3. Luke 18:18-22.

4. Saint Francis of Assisi, Brainy Quotes, Google search.

5. Ibid.

6. Ibid.

7. Francis of Assisi, *Canticle of The Sun, The Book of Common Worship,* The Presbyterian Church (U.S.A.), Westminster/John Knox Press: 1993, p. 800.

8. St Francis of Assisi, Brainy Quotes, Google search. op. cit.

9. Ibid. Biography section.

10. *Time Magazine,* Cover Story, March 25, 2013, pp. 18-25.

11. Augustine Thompson, O.P., *FRANCIS OF ASSISI, A NEW BIOGRA-PHY,* Cornell University Press, Ithaca and London: 2012, p. 36.

12. The Prayer of St. Francis, *The Book of Common Worship of The Presbyterian Church* (U.S.A.), op.cit. p.25.

Chapter Eight

The Hutterites

1. Exodus 20:13.

2. All information in this chapter is based on THE HUTTERITES IN NORTH AMERICA, John Hostetler and Gertrude Enders Huntington, Harcourt Brace College Publishers, Fort Worth, Philadelphia, San Diego, New York, Montreal, London, Sydney, Tokyo, 1996, 1980, Holt, Rinehart and Winston, Inc., and my personal experience and knowledge of the Hutterite community.

3. Ibid. p. 2.

4. Ibid. p. 100.

Chapter Nine

The Writings of Saint Paul, Romans 12:9-18

1. All references are contained in the text.

Chapter Ten

Ms. Betty Williams

1. Eli Wiesel, *LEGENDS OF OUR TIME*, Holt, Reinhart and Winston, New York: 1968, p. 180.

2. *Wikipedia, The Free Encyclopedia*, Betty Williams (Nobel Laureate), 5/3/12, p. 1 of 3.

3. Ibid.

4. Ibid.

5. *The Hartford Courant*, News In Education, "Meet A Change Maker, Betty Williams," March 13, 2012.

6. Numbers reported by Piers Morgan, CNN News, following the murder of seven people and the wounding of thirteen others at the University of California at Santa Barbara on May 23, 2014. See Chapter Six: "Guns in the Home" for a duplicate reporting of these numbers.

7. ABC News, Channel 8, New Haven, Ct., 6:00 P.M., July 5, 2014.

8. John D. Hicks, *THE FEDERAL UNION*, Houghton Mifflin Company, The Riverside Press, Cambridge, Massachusetts: 1952, p. 630.

Chapter Eleven

Carolyn McCarthy

1. Carolyn McCarthy, *Wikipedia, The Free Encyclopedia*, 5/3/12.
2. Ibid.
3. Ibid.
4. Ibid.
5. ABC News, Channel 8, New Haven, Connecticut, December 2012.
6. Colin Ferguson (Mass Murderer), *Wikipedia, The Free Encyclopedia*, 5/2/12.
7. Exodus 20:13.
8. See opening quotation, this chapter.

Chapter Twelve

The Golden Rule

1. Notes to Biblical references are included in the text.

Chapter Thirteen

Newtown

1. Both printed and television reporting of the Newtown, Connecticut, tragedy have been voluminous. *Time Magazine* devoted a cover story to the incident, *Time*, December 17, 2012. Local newspapers, indeed all media outlets, continue to cover any and all developments related to the Newtown disaster.
2. William Menninger, *The New York Times*, November 22, 1957.

Chapter Fourteen

Parenting for Peace

1. Eli Weisel, *LEGENDS OF OUR TIME*, Holt, Rinehart and Winston: 1968. p. 12.
2. Virginia Stair, Google earth, hug quotes, www.inspirationfalls.com.
3. Similar to a quotation by William Congreve (1670-1729), "The Mourning of The Bride," Act 1, Scene 1, found in *Tenth Edition of John Bartlett, Familiar Quotations*, 1919, p. 298.

4. John Erskine, *3000 QUOTATIONS ON CHRISTIAN THEMES*, op. cit. P. 97.

5. Frederich Wilhelm Nietzche, "Twilight of The Idols," Maxims and Missiles, paragraph 33. Found in Bartlett, op. cit. p. 727b.

Chapter Fifteen

A Children's Story

1. Biblical references are contained in the text.

2. The Presbyterian Hymnal, Westminster/John Knox Press, Louisville, 1990. Hymn written by Cecil Frances Alexander, 1848, p. 267 hymnal.

3. Story told by Rick Steves, *Travels in France,* CREATE TV.

Chapter Sixteen

Think about These Words

1. "GATES OF PRAYER." *The New Union Prayer Book,* Central Conference of American Rabbis, New York: 1973, p. 110.

2. John 18:11.

3. Charles Jeffreys (1807-1865) in Jeannot's Answer, Stanza 4, found John Bartlett, op. cit. p. 520.

4. Goodreads, online, Mother Teresa Quotes from her book *A SIMPLE FAITH.*

5. This is the ethical consequence of Augustine's assertion that a Christian has "dual" citizenship in the earthly city and the City of God. Discussed by Albert Terrill Rasmussen in *CHRISTIAN SOCIAL ETHICS,* Prentice Hall, Inc., Englewood Cliffs, New Jersey: 1956, 1958, p. 281.

6. Tim Russert, *BIG RUSS AND ME,* Miromax Books, Hyperion, New York: p. 333.

7. John Wesley, *Letters,* December 10, 1777. Bartlett, op. cit. p. 329.

8. St. Francis of Assisi, Brainy Quotes, online.

9. Matthew 5:9, from "The Sermon on the Mount."

10. The Rev. Dr. Martin Luther King Jr., Brainy Quotes, online.

11. John Lennon, Brainy Quotes, Google search.

12. Quoted by Charlie Rose, CBS News, February 2013.

13. John Lennon, Brainy Quotes, online.

14. William Targ, *Reader's Digest,* April 1947.

15. Isaiah 2:2-4.

16. Ephesians 4:22.

17. Dr. Peter Marshall, goodreads.com., Peter Marshall quotes.

18. Dr. Peter Masrshall, *The Study Bible Online,* Google search.

19. Mother Teresa, scrapbook.com, Google search.

20. Anonymous, *3000 QUOTATIONS ON CHRISTAIN THEMES,* op. cit. p. 17, para. 150.

21. Dag Hammerskjold, *3000 QUOTATIONS.* ibid., p. 3, para 14.

22. Mahatma Gandhi, May 8, 1937. Found in *Kiny Quotes on War and Peace,* p. 6 of 6.

23. Mario Cuomo, Interview, Encore NY RLTV, Channel 128, December 17, 2013, 1:00 P.M.

24. Nelson Mandela, Quotation reported on CBS News, 6:30 P.M., December 4, 2013.

25. Piers Morgan, CNN News, May 23, 2014.

26. William Gladstone, *Better World Quotes,* Googlesearch.

27. Mother Teresa, *THE JOY OF LOVING,* Viking Press, 1997, p. 163.